SEASONS
of
IRELAND

Thoughts, Poems, Proverbs & Recipes

JANE FADELY

SEASONS OF IRELAND
Thoughts, Poems, Proverbs & Recipes

Copyright © 2017 V. J. Fadely

ISBN-10: 1542598168
ISBN-13: 978-1542598163

Published in the USA - IREUSA Press (ireusapress@gmail.com)

First Printing February 18, 2017

Interior sketches are computer-generated images from photographs
Copyright © 2016 by V. J. Fadely

Just for you
Because you enjoy the changing seasons and love Ireland and all things Irish. Because you delight in even the smallest things when you are there, and when you've returned home find you've left a piece of your heart behind.

It is said God made the Italians for their beauty, the French for their fine food, the Swedes for their intelligence, and the Jews for religion. And on and on until finally, he looked at all he had created and said, "This is all very fine but no one is having fun. I guess I'll have to make me an Irishman." Or so the story goes...

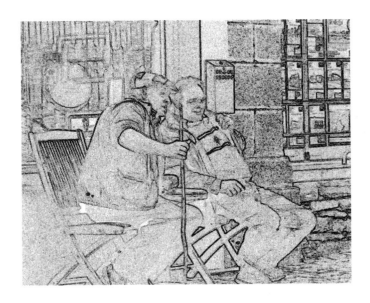

Foreword & Acknowledgments

During the three lovely years I had the good fortune to call Ireland my home, I became familiar with the seasons and watched them come and go with interest and fascination. Watching the ever-changing sky and admiring the flora and fauna became a daily pastime, and I seemed to become attuned to even the smallest signs hinting at the coming and going of each season. While many of my observations may well apply to many places around the globe, it is about Southwest Ireland I write, most specifically, the charming town of Kenmare and surrounds.

I got to thinking how many of us associate certain foods with specific seasons and decided including recipes for a few Irish dishes would add to the flavor (pun intended) of the book. The recipes were collected from dear friends and acquaintances, most of whom are Irish, and have been used with their permission. Without their kind contributions, I'd have had very few recipes!

I thank Bridget Haggerty and IrishCultureandCustoms.com, Betty Jeffries, Philomena Kelly, Deb Stephens Keogh, Katy Lucey and the Gougane Barra Hotel, Clare Smith and Ireland Unplugged Tours, and Jan Tebbutt. Sláinte!

An extra thank you to those who helped with converting the recipes from Irish-English to American-English! (Please see *Recipe Notes* on page 83 before trying the recipes.)

A special thanks goes to my dear mother, Pat Bearden, for proof-reading. Even at almost ninety years old her eyes - and likely her mind - are sharper than mine.

I hope readers will enjoy a little taste of a place dear to my heart and find this a pleasant and easy journey through the four seasons of Ireland - without need for umbrella or wellies. Ready? We're off!

Jane

♣

On an unknown path every foot is slow.
- Irish Proverb

Passing Seasons

My time in beautiful Ireland too soon ran its course
Seasons coming and going
With a certain and too swift force.
I watched the sea waves swell and crash,
Smelled the sweet scent of burning peat
Saw leaves turning and falling,
Laying scattered at my feet.
I listened to raging winter storms
Great winds howling through the night
Watched cheerful fires chase away the gloom,
Bringing warmth and light.
I saw spring come 'round the corner,
Flowers blooming in colorful displays
Then the lush greens and growth of summer
And the sunshine of long twilight days.
The Irish people and the land became so very dear
Parting was such deep sorrow
And I left with a heavy heart and a tear.
But I smile when I remember those days on cliff and shore
And the rainbows o'er the hilltops
And the mossy forest floor
The Irish wit and wisdom, the laughter and the smiles
The bodhrán beats, and fiddle tunes,
The magic of the Emerald Isle.
I have memories aplenty, in my heart they'll always be
Those years in dear old Ireland
Forever a part of me.

♣

May you always have walls for the wind,
A roof for the rain, and tea beside the fire.
- Irish Blessing

CONTENTS

Winter - 1

Spring - 21

Summer - 39

Autumn - 59

Did You Know? - 79

Recipe Notes - 83

Recipe Index - 85

Photo List - 86

WINTER

Firelight will not let you read fine stories
but it will warm you
and you won't see the dust on the floor.
- Irish Proverb

A misty winter brings a pleasant spring, a pleasant winter a misty spring.
- Irish Saying

WINTER

Winter is a time of thinking and rethinking. Reconnecting. Planning. Resting. A time for warm fires, hot whiskey, camaraderie in the local pubs, and empty village streets. Rain. Wind. Frost. Sleet pinging against the windows and sliding down in lazy, icy rivulets. *Closed for the Season* signs. Heavier jackets, scarves wound tightly around necks, and knit hats. Cleaning out the wood stove or fireplace and keeping the indoor wood basket filled become part of the daily routine and are chores elevated to a position of higher priority.

If winter was human, it would be solemn, stern, strong and moody; sometimes fierce, but perhaps misunderstood and not necessarily as unkind as it often seems. Something like a crotchety old uncle once full of life and vigor who, in his waning years, has let past injustices, missed opportunities, and hurts weigh him down. He rails against growing older, his real self hidden under his burdens and discontent, yet if you spend enough time in his company, you find flashes of his old warmth and charm.

Days are short and fires are often lit by mid-afternoon before darkness descends and the real chill sets in. The sweet smell of turf smoke drifts from chimneys, no bother to the ever-present rooks and jackdaws perched on rooftops and along the telephone wires. They scold with their harsh, insistent cries as though proclaiming their dominance and their enthusiasm for the coming of winter.

The earth tones of the valleys and hillsides become more prominent as the golden and crimson autumn colors fade. Once dull green or dusky brown ferns turn a darker, brittle brown and curl in on themselves. Until the first frosts, much of the grass stays green, but in a less vibrant shade. In early winter gorse still shows its gold, but is a ragged shadow of its autumn self. Blackberries shrivel and die on the vines and migratory birds make haste to fly south.

The brightly painted buildings found in most Irish towns and villages loom larger and brighter, looking naked without the flowers, outdoor tables, and sun umbrellas to hide behind. But once the eye adjusts, even those in need of a spring paint job bring welcome color to winter's duller palette.

Skies can be dull, gray, the blue covered with dark flat clouds sagging heavily with rain, the quiet gloom before the storm. The red berries of cotoneaster and holly stand out like Christmas lights against the muted landscape, blazing against the dark trees, black rocks and gunmetal gray skies.

And then the clouds swell and burst open and the rain falls, and the winds begin to blow, rattling the early winter trees' nearly bare branches. In their final shuddering, the trees stop resisting and shake off the last of their autumn leaves like a dog shaking water off after a swim.

Day by day darkness lengthens and deepens. Morning frost coats grass and ivy and those hardy flowers still growing along stone walls, oblivious to winter. Colors are further muted but the sun catches and sparkles on the frosty vegetation making it look like sugar decorations on a cake.

Sometimes a nice light snowfall sprinkles the barren landscape with a dusting of white, settling more heavily in the hills and mountains, but more often than not it is rain that falls, lashing against the window pane, forming deepening puddles in the back garden, dripping off the roof, and flowing down the streets in miniature rushing rivers.

The colder temperatures and winter winds cause the pace of walking to be brisk, yet it is a time when people stop for a chat when they run into someone they know on the street – or someone they don't – because everyone has more time now. But they don't linger as long as they might have in summer sunshine or on a crisp autumn day. The wind whistling in their ears, the cold seeping into their bones and the rain dripping off the shop awnings are all good reminders to keep moving.

Mid-winter can bring those kind of days when, if you don't have to go anywhere, you probably don't. You might poke your head out the door to assess the weather and watch as your breath hangs in clouds in the cold air, but then you close the door with a shiver and return to the fire, keeping it stoked, perhaps lighting a candle or two as further cheer against the gloom. You curl up with a cup of tea and a good book or an old classic film, and nestle together if you're part of a pair, or into a comfy old quilt if you're not. It is this sort of day, with indoors in sharp contrast to outdoors, when one can truly understand and appreciate the meaning of the word *cozy*.

As winter advances, shop and pub windows come alive with the twinkling lights of Christmas, miniature trees shining with silver and red decorations, boughs of greenery, and sprigs of holly. Pub fires give off a rosy glow and patrons gather to sit or stand at the bar, their laughing and chatting voices steaming up the windows and creating frosty backdrops for the strings of festive lights glowing in welcome. Musicians who have been scarce for awhile, perhaps enjoying a holiday in sunny Spain, begin gathering again and the music sessions resume, welcome and enjoyable entertainment on a cold winter's evening or gray Sunday afternoon.

When the winds gather strength over the Atlantic Ocean and blow easterly in strong gusts, chasing away the last traces of gray, ushering in a bright, fresh, winter blue sky, people look up, blinking and squinting, and smile broadly.

Though often difficult to determine how to dress for the changing weather in Ireland, in winter there is no question as to whether a coat is needed, and quite likely a warm scarf and hat, no matter how brightly the sun might be shining on any given day. Enjoy the sunshine while it is here, then warm your hands with a hot whiskey or a cup of tea, whether in the corner pub over a chat and a few laughs with friends, or by your own home fire.

There is much talk of the weather, but also of spring as though it somehow brings warmth. And when the weather is very bad, a right "dirty" old day, when the wind seems to blow right through you, the rain stings your face, and your fingers are numb with cold, there is always someone ready with the reminder, "Spring is just around the corner!" And it is, of course - it is.

♣

Newgrange at Brú na Bóinne

Newgrange is the largest of the passage tombs at Brú na Bóinne. Constructed over 5,000 years ago, it is older than the Egyptian pyramids. On the six days around winter solstice in December, weather permitting, a shaft of sunlight illuminates the narrow passageway and inner chamber of the tomb at exactly four minutes after sunrise. Even from the outside the tomb is a mysterious, awe-inspiring and thought-provoking place, in any season. My visit inspired my imagination and the following poem.

Imagining Winter Solstice at Newgrange

The sun follows its sure path
Seeking the target
Blind to all distractions
A shaft of brilliance
Illuminating the cold stone passageway
Hungrily consuming the dark
On its familiar 5,000 year old journey
Bringing light to winter
Clearing the path for spring
Reaching its destination with joy
And reverence -
Then bows its ancient head
In pious prayer.

Winter Trees

Autumn leaves have blown away
Tree branches now dark and lean
But they are in good company
Among the steady evergreen.
Together they all sigh and sway
As winter comes to call
The frigid air and chill winds
Seem not to bother them at all.

Wishing for Spring

When the cold chills us through
And our bones are weary
And from looking at winter's landscape,
Our eyes grow bleary
We think of spring and seeing the green grass grow
Of flowers blooming in gardens
And along the hedgerow
The rainbows and song birds
And the earth's scent, so sweet
And the warmth that floods us from head to feet
As we walk down a lane, faces turned to the sun
We'll smile and say, "Ah, now winter is done!"

Recipes for Winter

Liz's Porter Cake

Beef & Guinness Stew

O'Sullivan's Christmas Pudding

Irish Coffee

Hot Whiskey

Enough and no waste is as good as a feast.
- Irish Proverb

LIZ'S PORTER CAKE *(P. 12)*

My dear friend and once sometimes neighbor, Betty (O'Sullivan) Jeffries, originally of Kenmare, County Kerry provided this recipe. She remembers when she was a child helping her mother Liz make this cake, in the old cottage which her family still owns, a few doors down from where I once lived. A traditional Irish cake, good any time of year, but a favorite at Christmastime.

BEEF & GUINNESS STEW *(P. 14)*

This is good old American beef stew with an Irish twist. I learned how to make a version of it from my mother, minus the Guinness. This is one of those dishes that really tastes even better when reheated and is delicious served with a crusty, hearty bread such as Irish soda bread or brown bread (see Autumn Recipes). Traditionally, in Ireland the dish is made without the potatoes, then served on a bed of mashed potatoes. No one says - certainly not the Irish - you can't do both!

O'SULLIVAN'S CHRISTMAS PUDDING *(P. 16)*

Winter brings Christmas and it's time to make Christmas cakes and puddings! The Irish version of American fruitcake, Christmas pudding takes some time. This recipe is also from Betty. She tells me her family enjoyed an 18-month old edition of one of these puddings this past Christmas. The longer you keep it, the better it is - say those who are connoisseurs! Now roll up your sleeves, gather all willing helpers, and unless there might be a fiddle or whistle player sitting in the corner, put on some Christmas music, and get started on pudding making!

IRISH COFFEE *(P. 18)*

You can't have a book which includes any Irish recipes without a recipe for the famed Irish Coffee now, can you? The key here is to get the cream to float on top as long as possible without melting into the coffee so you first taste the cold cream and then the hot coffee and whiskey. A poorly made Irish Coffee is like a badly poured pint of Guinness - why waste the time and the calories?

HOT WHISKEY *(P. 19)*

Whiskey lover or not, it makes no difference. There is nothing like a good hot whiskey on a frigid winter's day. It will chase away the cold and damp and if you're feeling a bit under the weather, ask nearly any Irishman: a few of these are sure to soothe your aches and pains, help you breathe easier, and generally perk you up. Ah, sure, you'll be singing "Molly Malone" with the best of them in no time!

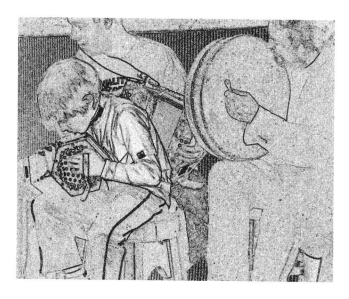

Good humor comes from the kitchen.
- Irish Proverb

LIZ'S PORTER CAKE
Betty (O'Sullivan) Jeffries

Betty is one of my contributors who weighs her dry ingredients. Both weight and volume measurements (in brackets) are included where applicable - your choice!

Ingredients:

4 oz [1 C] self-rising flour
4oz [just under 1 C] all purpose flour
1 tspn baking soda
2 tspn mixed spice [pumpkin spice in the USA]
pinch of salt
4 oz [1/2 C or 1 stick] butter
6 oz [3/4 C packed] brown sugar
1 lb [3 C] mixed fruit (raisins and any other dried fruits of your choice)
2 oz [1/3 C] candied cherries
2 eggs
10-12 oz [12 oz bottle] Guinness Draught

Directions:

1. Preheat oven to 375 deg. F.
2. In a saucepan heat the butter, sugar, fruit, and Guinness. Bring all the ingredients to a boil, reduce heat and simmer for about 10-12 mins. or until the fruit has plumped up. Cool.
3. When the mixture has cooled, add eggs and beat well by hand.
4. Sift dry ingredients into the fruit mixture; fold in.
5. Pour into 8" round parchment-lined baking pan and bake for 1 hour to 1 hour 15 mins. Cake is done when toothpick inserted into center comes out clean.

Notes:

- As an option, before baking the cake, sprinkle some course/raw brown sugar or chopped nuts - or both - over the top.

I'll put the kettle on for tea -
Won't you please slice a piece of that porter cake for me?

You don't know what's in the pot
until the lid is lifted.
- Irish Proverb

BEEF & GUINNESS STEW

This is easy to make. Adjust both the ingredients and quantities as desired, for more or less meat-to-veggie ratio. A great make-ahead dish and even better when reheated.

Ingredients:

2 lbs chuck roast or stewing beef, cut into 1-2" chunks
4-6 C potatoes and carrots cut into chunks
1/4 C chopped onion, fresh or dried
4-6 C beef stock
1/4-1/2 C diced celery
1/4 C diced parsley, fresh or dried
1/4-1/2 C ketchup
flour for coating beef, seasoned with salt and pepper
1 [12 oz.] bottle Guinness Extra Stout
dash or two of Worcester Sauce
(You may add additional seasonings of your choice - e.g., thyme, garlic - and any other vegetables desired. Left-over pot roast makes this a super easy dish!)

Directions:

1. Coat the beef in the seasoned flour mixture and brown in a little oil. If using your stew pot to do this, leave the beef in the pan, otherwise transfer to the pot you will use.
2. Saute onions (unless using dried) and celery in same pan, then pour in a little of the Guinness and scrape to get the browned bits from the meat off the bottom of the pan.
3. In your cooking pot, add the browned bits, and all ingredients except the carrots and potatoes.

4. Cover and simmer on stove top or in oven at about 325 deg. for at least 2 hrs, until beef begins to get tender.
5. Add in carrots and additional liquid as needed.
6. When carrots are semi-cooked, add potatoes.
7. Continue cooking about 30 minutes more until meat is tender and vegetables are cooked.
8. For a thicker broth, start with (or add in later) a simple gravy, or use a bit of cornstarch or packaged gravy mix.

Notes:

- Canned or dried French Onion soup may be used as an alternative to some or all of the chopped dried or fresh onion and beef stock, if you wish.

- If you'd like to add the potatoes and carrots at the same time, just cut the carrots much smaller and the potatoes in larger chunks.

A cold wind blows and the rain beats its staccato rhythm on the roof, but the fire is warm, you've a cup of tea at hand, and the stew is simmering on the stove.

O'SULLIVAN'S CHRISTMAS PUDDING
Betty Jeffries

This recipe makes two puddings. If you plan to keep them beyond a few months, add a few tablespoons of liquor every 4-6 months and keep tightly wrapped in parchment paper and foil. Again, volume measurements are in brackets.

Ingredients:

4 oz [7/8 C+1-1/2 tspn] all-purpose flour
1/2 tspn salt
2 tspn mixed spice (pumpkin spice in USA)
2 tspn cinnamon
2 tspn nutmeg
2 oz [5/8 C] ground almonds
8 oz [1 C, packed] dark brown sugar
8 oz [1 C] butter plus extra for greasing bowls and parchment paper
12 oz [5-7/8 C] fresh white bread crumbs
6 eggs, beaten
juice and zest of 1 orange
1 large apple, peeled, cored and grated
10 oz [1-7/8 C] each: sultanas, raisins
8 oz [1-1/2 C] each: currants, chopped dates
4 oz [3/4 C] candied cherries, chopped
4 oz [7/8 C] candied mixed peel
10-12 oz [1 bottle] Guinness Draught
12-16 Tbspn liquor (rum, brandy or whiskey)

Directions:

1. Soak fruit in 6-8 tablespoons liquor for 24-48 hrs.
2. Cream butter and sugar and add beaten eggs, flour, spices and some breadcrumbs alternately.

3. Add the fruit, the rest of the breadcrumbs, and the Guinness and stir well.

4. Grease two 1.5 quart (min. 40 oz. each) bowls.

5. Divide mixture between the two bowls and cover with greased parchment paper, then foil, and tie down securely with string.

6. Steam for 6 hrs. min. No steamer? Set each bowl into a pot with a tight fitting lid. and fill with enough water to reach about half-way up the sides of the bowl. Bring to a boil, cover and reduce to a simmer. Add water as needed.

7. Remove pot lid(s) and pudding coverings; cool.

8. Pour 3-4 tablespoons of liquor over the top of each pudding, cover with fresh parchment paper and foil, tie up tightly with string and store for at least 2 months.

9. Re-steam for 2 hours before serving.

Notes:

- You may use any combination of dried and candied fruits, but keep the total and the ratio the same (candied fruit about 1-1/2 cups, dried fruit about 6-1/2 cups).

- If you plan to keep the pudding for more than a few months, be sure to "feed" it with 2-3 tablespoons of your chosen liquor about every 3 months and keep tightly wrapped. Giving one as a gift? Do give the recipient care and feeding instructions along with the pudding!

Happy Christmas!

IRISH COFFEE

Make sure the coffee is hot and the cream cold. Heavy cream will give you the best results (over spray or regular whipped cream). Yum!

Ingredients:

1.5 oz Irish whiskey
1/2-1 tspn brown or white sugar (to taste)
freshly brewed *hot* black coffee
heavy cream, lightly whipped and sweetened, if desired

Directions:

1. Pour the sugar, whiskey and very hot coffee into the bottom of a heat-proof glass mug. Stir.

2. Top with *cold* cream. If cream isn't whipped, pouring it over an inverted teaspoon held over the top of the mug will help it settle gently on top.

Drink, enjoy, and repeat.

HOT WHISKEY

This will warm you from the inside out!

Ingredients:
1.5 oz Irish whiskey
1/2 slice of fresh lemon
5 whole cloves
1 tspn sugar (more or less to taste)
boiling water

Directions:

1. Stick the cloves into the fruit part of the lemon slice.
2. Put sugar and clove-studded lemon into clear glass mug.
3. Add the whiskey.
4. Add boiling water to fill the mug; stir.

This would go nicely with a slice of Liz's Porter Cake if you're feeling more adventurous than a cup of tea!

What butter and whiskey will not cure
there's no cure for.
- Irish Proverb

*May you have a full moon on a dark night
and the road downhill all the way to your door.*
- *Irish Blessing*

SPRING

*Many a sudden change
takes place on a spring day.*
-Irish Proverb

"If it doesn't rain between the showers, it'll be a fine day!" - *Irish Saying*

SPRING

*I*t *was one of those March days when the sun shines hot and the wind blows cold: when it is summer in the light, and winter in the shade.* (Charles Dickens, *Great Expectations*) Mr. Dickens wasn't Irish, but England's weather is much like Ireland's and he perfectly captured an Irish spring with those well-written words.

Spring is fanciful, whimsical, innocent, and seems to be forever changing its mind. It sometimes has trouble co-existing with the cool air left behind by winter, but still remains cheerful and playful most days. There is good reason for the Irish saying, "If you don't like the weather, wait five minutes - it will change!" This seems especially true in springtime. But there is overall a shift in the air, a brightness, and the days begin to grow longer, allowing the sun to gather more strength and cast its rays upon the still hibernating bulbs and buds, coaxing them to eventually emerge as the opening act for spring, despite the chill which stubbornly remains.

Just as Ireland has rightfully earned its reputation for quick-change weather, so, too, its reputation for rainbows. The regular rainfall, combined with the periods of sunshine often even on the rainiest of days, are perfect conditions for rainbows to appear. Spring is perhaps peak rainbow season and seeing a double rainbow arching over rolling green fields is not uncommon, yet it is rare enough to always be a glorious sight to behold.

When the calendar says spring but the too cool temperatures say winter, tiny green shoots of early spring flowers poke through the soil. Defying the cold, snow drops, crocus, and bright daffodils bloom and bob their pretty heads in the sun and in the rain. Songbirds gather in the trees and in gardens, singing with almost hyper-enthusiasm, welcoming spring.

With the sun shining, the birds singing, the flowers beginning to bloom, and the very smell of green in the air, the urge is strong to tear off heavy winter jackets and let the sunshine find your skin before it is quite time to do so.

"Summer is coming!" becomes the standard and oft-repeated phrase, no matter how cold the temperature. In fact, the colder it is, the more often and emphatically this is said, as though positive thinking might help the weather to warm. And who knows? It surely couldn't hurt.

On any bright sunny day, no matter how cool, people are out in shirt-sleeves washing windows, sweeping front steps and walkways, tidying garden hedges and planting beds. Soon, lawn chairs are pulled from garages and out buildings, freed of cobwebs and dust, and arranged in the garden at the ready for outdoor gatherings. Chances are those gatherings might have to be moved indoors to escape rain or cold, but the Irish do not waste time worrying about "what if - ?" There are so many other wonderful things to do.

In towns and cities flower vendors display multi-colored blooms on street corners and weekly outdoor markets begin to grow larger. Buildings stand fresh and bright in their new coats of paint, proudly wearing their hanging baskets and window boxes of plants and flowers like precious jewelry.

Green thumbs itch to get into flower gardens to add more color, to ready the soil for planting vegetables and flowers; to dig, to coax, to clip, and then to enjoy. If your garden includes violas, chances are they have weathered the winter and are still blooming, their sweet little faces belying their amazing toughness.

Then one day you notice a distinct change, no longer just a promise, a hint, a prelude, but the real thing. The temperature has caught up with the season. The air is finally warmer and the landscape rejoices, alive with color everywhere you look.

The unfurling of majestic purple stalks of Iris seem to be a royal announcement of the official arrival of spring. Wild cherry, apple and hawthorn trees explode in pink and white blossoms, impressive, fluffy, playful splashes of alternately vivid and soft colors. Patches of bluebells grace the green and fields are covered in tiny daisies. When viewed from a distance, the countryside looks like a beautiful impressionist painting.

The short life of dandelions plays out before your eyes. Popping up overnight and covering the grass like a yellow carpet, they quickly go to seed, turning to white nearly invisible puff-balls. And even if you've been quick enough to pick a few and make a wish, there are many more for the breeze to take, lifting the almost weightless seeds and filling the air with millions of floating unwished wishes.

There is an explosion in the baby animal population; lambs, calves and colts are everywhere, some sticking close to their mothers, others more brave, frolicking across the grass, playing, exploring, and chasing birds.

The feel of finally walking unencumbered by winter wear is freeing and delightful. People smile more and stand straighter, no longer hunched against the cold and wind. And though they haven't always the time, they look for excuses to stop outdoors for a chat, to linger in the presence of the sunshine and flowers, in the fresh new world taking shape, a world emerging like a butterfly from the confining cocoon of winter.

With the coming of spring, so too come longer days, longer walks, deeper breathing, and faces frequently turned skyward at any appearance of the sun, no matter how brief.

In the woods and on high mountain passes, spring rainfall has engorged rivers and streams and created silver waterfalls glinting in the sun, cascading down high rocky cliffs to the valley floor, some to join quiet pools, others to continue their journey in a murmuring, gently tumbling brook or a noisy, racing river, all the way to the sea.

Spring is a time for going outdoors on clear nights to look at the moon and the stars, for quiet walks through the woods to hunt shamrocks and see tiny wildflowers and new growth on trees and bushes. Keep your eyes open for faeries and leprechauns because surely if you're going to see one, it would be in a mossy forest in the springtime when the shamrocks are in bloom. Wherever you are, whatever you are doing, pause, breathe deeply, listen, look, relax. No matter how cool the air, spring will find you.

♣

Time

Time in Ireland
Seems sometimes not to exist
It is a seamless mix
Of green fields and fresh air
Peat fires and pints
Especially in the spring.
Shamrocks and daisies and yellow gorse
Join with baby animals
To dance across the landscape,
Sea cliffs and friendly faces
Melting into the mist and the music.
Ancient stone walls, ring forts
And crumbling castles
Provide a framework, cradling us
As we walk, feel, laugh, breathe
In peace
Drifting along to the end of the day
To watch the colors of the sunset unfold
And wash over the land.
While the songbirds sleep
We are sprinkled with rain and stars,
And watched over
By the man in the moon
Gazing down as he does
With his gentle Mona Lisa smile.

There's a lot of weather in a March day.
- Irish Saying

Recipes for Spring

Pendy's Potato Cakes

Clare's Irish Stew

Colcannon

Chocolate Guinness Cake

Laughter is brightest where food is best.
- Irish Proverb

PENDY'S POTATO CAKES *(P. 32)*

There are so many O'Sullivans in Co. Kerry, many of the families have nicknames. The potato cake recipe is from the "Pendy" O'Sullivan's, passed down through the generations. Just reading it makes my mouth water! The O'Sullivan's made the potato pancakes with leftover mashed potatoes. If you've even the smallest bit of Irish in you, then surely you've some leftover mashed potatoes?

CLARE'S IRISH STEW *(P. 33)*

Clare Smith and partner Dezy Walls have a lovely bed and breakfast, Thidwick, on the Ring of Kerry. Situated above Derrynane Bay, the spacious yet cozy house gives superior and dramatic views of the coastline. They also operate Ireland Unplugged Tours. [irelandunpluggedtours.com] Lucky guests enjoy the ambiance, views, and fabulous breakfasts of the B&B and the adventure and fun of touring the Ring of Kerry with Clare and Dezy. Clare's Irish stew is a traditional favorite and she has no doubt pleased many a guest with it!

COLCANNON *(P. 35)*

Colcannon is the anglicized version of the Irish word for "white-headed cabbage." A potato and cabbage dish, it is popular in Ireland. The recipe included here is one I found in a magazine some years ago. It's a good dish, easy to make, and something authentic to take to a St. Patrick's Day party!

CHOCOLATE GUINNESS CAKE *(P. 36)*

This recipe was given to me several years ago by a Canadian friend, Deb Stephens Keogh, a fellow Ireland-lover. Deb and I met on a trip to Ireland in 2009, the first visit for both of us. We each returned several times thereafter. After one such holiday, Deb brought back this Chocolate Guinness cake recipe. After another holiday she brought back her own Irishman! The two recently wed and I can picture them sitting in their garden among the spring flowers exchanging words of love and laughter, eating chocolate Guinness cake and sipping Deb's favorite (and mine), Barry's Gold Blend tea...

A cabin with plenty of food
is better than a hungry castle.
- Irish Proverb

♣
PENDY'S POTATO CAKES
Betty Jeffries

This recipe is not for the fried potato "pancakes" you might be familiar with. These combine flour and egg with the potatoes and are baked in the oven, giving them a nice soft, fluffy texture.

Ingredients:
8 oz [2 C] self-rising flour
1/2 tspn salt
12 -16 oz [3-4 C] mashed potatoes
1 egg, beaten
2 heaping Tbspn butter
1/4-1/2 C milk, as needed

Directions:
1. Preheat oven to 375 deg. F.
2. Place flour and salt in a bowl with the butter and using your fingers, rub the butter into the flour.
3. Rub or fork in the potato.
4. Make a well in center and mix in beaten egg with a fork.
5. Add milk as necessary to make a soft pliable dough.
6. Place on a floured board and knead until dough is smooth.
7. Roll out to 1/2 inch thickness. Cut into rounds about 3 inches.
8. Place on baking sheet and bake for about 30 minutes.
9. After removing from oven wrap in a clean tea towel to keep them soft and warm.
10. Split and butter and eat while hot.

Good in any season but would be a lovely addition to Easter brunch or a St. Patrick's Day spread!

CLARE'S IRISH STEW
Clare Smith

A good make-ahead dish when company's coming!

Ingredients:

6-8 lamb chops for stewing
2 medium onions, chopped
2 cloves garlic, finely chopped
1 stalk of celery, diced
baby potatoes or potatoes cut into chunks
carrots cut into chunks
1-2 C vegetable broth
cooking oil
1 Tbspn tomato paste
pinch of rosemary
pinch of thyme
1 tspn mustard
1 tspn parsley
salt & pepper to taste

Directions:

1. Sauté onions, garlic and celery, then remove from pan.
2. Dredge lamb in a mixture of flour, salt and pepper and brown in a little oil, then remove from pot.
3. Deglaze pot by adding a few tablespoons of water and scraping the drippings.
4. Add tomato paste, a pinch of fresh or dried rosemary and thyme, and salt & pepper to taste.
5. Return other ingredients to pan and add enough vegetable broth (or water) so lamb is about 3/4 covered.
6. Cover and simmer over low heat for 1 hour.

7. Add desired amount of potatoes and carrots, making sure there is enough liquid in the pot. (You may want to cut the carrots smaller than the potatoes or add in earlier unless you like them *al dente*.)
8. Continue to simmer *gently*, lid slightly ajar, for 1 hour.
9. Toward end of cooking time add mustard and parsley.

Hm-m-m... something smells delicious!

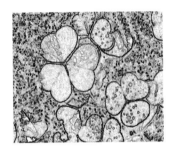

A stew boiled is a stew spoiled.
- Irish Saying

COLCANNON

This is obviously an Americanized colcannon recipe as it uses American-style bacon, different than Irish bacon. Irish bacon is very lean, more like Canadian Bacon. You may wish to use a bit of both. The onion and cabbage will benefit from being sauteed in those tasty American bacon drippings you can't get from Canadian or Irish bacon.

Ingredients:

2 1/2 lbs potatoes, peeled and cubed
4 slices bacon (American-style)
1/2 a small head of cabbage, chopped finely
1 large onion, chopped finely
1/2 C milk
1/4 C butter, melted
salt and pepper to taste

Directions:

1. Boil potatoes for 15 to 20 minutes, until tender.
2. Place bacon in a large, deep skillet and fry over medium high heat until evenly cooked and crispy. Drain, reserving drippings, crumble and set aside.
3. Saute the cabbage and onion in the bacon drippings until soft and translucent. Putting a lid on the pan helps the vegetables cook faster.
4. Drain potatoes, mash with milk, season with salt and pepper. Fold in the bacon, cabbage, and onions, then transfer the mixture to a large serving bowl.
5. Pour melted butter into a well in the center of the potatoes and serve immediately.

Potatoes, butter, and bacon - how can you go wrong?!

CHOCOLATE GUINNESS CAKE

Deb Keogh (obtained from someone, somewhere,
during her travels across the Irish countryside!)

*This is a tasty, moist, rich cake and you needn't be a Guinness drinker to
enjoy it.*

Ingredients:

1 C Guinness Extra Stout
1/2 C butter, cubed
2 C granulated white sugar
3/4 C unsweetened cocoa
2 eggs, beaten
2/3 C sour cream
3 tspn vanilla extract
2 C all-purpose flour
1-1/2 tspn baking soda

Icing: 2-1/2 C confectioners sugar; 16 oz (2 pkgs) cream cheese;
1 C whipping cream

Cake Directions:

1. Preheat oven to 350 deg. F. and grease a 9-in. spring-form pan. Line the bottom with parchment paper.
2. In a small saucepan, heat Guinness and butter until butter is melted. Remove from heat.
3. Whisk in granulated sugar and cocoa until blended.
4. Combine eggs, sour cream and vanilla in a separate bowl, then whisk into Guinness mixture.
5. Combine flour and baking soda in another bowl, then whisk into liquid mixture until smooth. Pour batter into prepared pan.
6. Bake at 350 deg. F for 45-50 minutes or until a toothpick inserted near the center comes out clean.

7. Cool completely in pan on a wire rack. Remove sides of pan when cake is cooled.

Icing Directions:

1. Beat sugar and cream cheese with an electric mixer.
2. Add the whipping cream in *slowly* (may not need full cup) until the frosting is glossy and thick enough to form peaks.
3. Spread on the top of the cake so it resembles a just poured, creamy pint of Guinness.

Notes:

• For an extra-rich flavor, substitute some of the white sugar with brown sugar and add 1/2 C chopped dark chocolate to the cake batter.

Enjoy - and remember: Guinness makes you strong!

A good word never broke a tooth.
- *Irish Proverb*

SUMMER

To sit in the shade on a fine day, and look upon verdure is the most perfect refreshment.
-Jane Austen

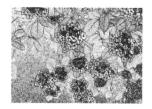

S U M M E R

Summer... a laughing, dancing flower child in a long flowing dress, a wreath of flowers encircling her head, a daisy chain around her neck, filled with boundless energy and good cheer. She skips and twirls along the streets and across the fields and sandy beaches, pausing occasionally to dip her bare toes into the sea, or rest briefly on an old stone wall to better hear the birds sing, or in the doorway of an ancient castle where she lifts her long hair to let the cool breeze brush her neck.

If spring is alive with color, summer is spring on steroids. Colors seem to explode before your very eyes, ivy grows as if on an urgent mission, and flowers sprout and bloom overnight. Blossoms and greenery cascade down the sides of hanging baskets and window boxes, wildflowers cover the fields and line the roadways, gardens grow in bountiful, swirling, varying hues of pinks and reds, deep violet, palest creams and lavenders, brilliant orange, and bright yellow. Most gardens are not the meticulously shaped and trimmed uniform beds you might see on a grand estate, but rather lushly growing, intertwining places of wild beauty where birds like to sing and butterflies alight.

Pockets of soil in the nooks and crannies of old stone walls are perfect beds for wildflower seeds riding the wind, and the blooms appear to sprout from the stones themselves.

An Irish summer is rarely a lazing-in-the-backyard-with-a-glass-of-cold-lemonade-beneath-a-shady-tree-to-escape-the-heat affair. And that's not because lemonade as Americans know it doesn't really exist in Ireland. No, it's because the temperatures are generally too cool and the sun too fickle; one never knows when it might rain or when an almost icy breeze will spring up, making shirt-sleeve weather suddenly call for a jacket.

You won't find parched lawns and heat that bakes the earth causing it to harden and crack, or heavy tropical humidity of the kind that seems to suck the breath out of you. These things are not part of an Irish summer, but there is no doubt the season does exist, and is most welcome in Ireland, rain or shine.

The daylight hours are long, stretching into the night. Sunset and twilight are slow, lingering affairs, coloring the sky with beautiful streaks of pink and red and gold, deepening to magenta, then darkest purple, and finally, reluctantly melting into the velvet black of night.

Morning comes very early and quite likely far before you are ready to awaken, but ready or not, if you are a country-dweller, the roosters will let you know as five o-clock and sunrise approaches. If you live in town you'll get to sleep a little later until you're awakened by the rumble, bang and clang of Guinness and Murphy's trucks and their drivers on their morning mission, picking up empty kegs and delivering fresh ones to the pubs. If you live on the edge of town, well lucky you! You'll have the rooster for an alarm and the trucks as backup, like a long snooze button. But arise! It is summer and time to greet the day.

As the sleepy streets awaken, pubs and cafes set out tables and chairs on the sidewalks, indeed, sometimes even on the street, where patrons can enjoy a coffee, a pint, or a meal in the open air. Shop doors are propped open and merchandise hung outside. Purple striped baby outfits so adorable you must stop to admire them, lace table runners, Irish linen tea towels, and brilliantly colored scarves all dance and sway in the breeze like flags.

People stroll, stop to chat, duck in and out of shops. Voices mix with the tinkle of wind chimes hanging from shop fronts, the music regularly coming from the pubs, and the tunes played by buskers on street corners, young teens with hope and excitement in their eyes and older, more practical folks, eyes not quite as bright, but filled with wisdom, singing the songs they've sung for years, instrument cases open on the sidewalk, hoping to collect a few euros.

Streets are soon clogged with traffic, locals and tourists alike, everyone intent on being out and about, to catch their share of summer. The chance of rain or cool air does nothing to decrease the eager enthusiasm. The very possibility of change, of sunshine or a warming in the temperature, is alone strong enough motivation to be out and about. It is summer; one must not miss a beautiful day should it suddenly materialize.

And, oh, when a true summer day appears its beauty and softness nearly take your breath away. The high clouds are a fluffy, pristine white, lazily drifting across a tender blue sky, the sun dazzling in its brilliance. The stronger summer sun warms the air, melting the cool away. It is on a day like this when you might hear the expression, "The sun's splittin' the stones!" (i.e.,

"It's so hot you can fry an egg on the sidewalk!"). It isn't truly hot, but it feels that way when cooler temps are the norm year-round.

Bees drone among the flowers, blossoms sway in the breeze, and trees are lushly green. Roadside vegetation is so thick in places you can't see the fields or stone walls beyond, the trees, tangles of blackberry vines and ivy, tall grasses and ferns weaving together to form a united summer blockade. Birds soar and flit from tree to tree, their music filling the air, a wonderful blend of enthusiastic and melodic songs, a perfect summer symphony.

Summer is fair and festival season in Ireland, many held annually for hundreds of years. There are story telling, music, and film festivals, literary festivals, walking festivals, and food festivals, many continuing into the autumn months, each one unique, and all adding to the celebratory and joyous mood of Ireland in summer.

Open-air markets continue to expand as days grow warmer. Visiting one is like a trip to another world, a maze of narrow avenues lined with pretty colors, shapes and textures, interesting sounds, and wonderful scents. In addition to farm produce you might find blocks and wheels of a wide-variety of cheeses, fragrant home-baked breads and sweets, local honey, racks of vintage clothing, hand-made jewelry glittering in the sunshine, and hand-crafted pottery in deep-hued blues and earthy, rich browns and speckled reds. If you think you smell coffee, you're probably right. Just follow your nose until you find the right stand. With a little bit of Irish luck, a neighboring stand is selling crepes made to order.

Whether you buy anything or just enjoy the ambiance, a trip to the market is also a chance to chat with friends, neighbors, and strangers alike, and prolong your time in the lovely summer sunshine, but even if it isn't market day you can still enjoy a pleasant walk through town. You're sure to encounter friends as well as at least one stranger in need of information or directions, shopkeepers sweeping the sidewalks in front of their establishments, and maybe an empty chair at an outside table where you can stop for tea or a pint.

Outside of town, streams and rivers are smaller than they were in spring and play a lighter, softer tune as they make their way through fields and into the woods, along the shadowy forest floor among the evergreens and thickets of ferns and other underbrush. The water runs crystal clear, revealing the smooth polished stones beneath the surface.

Birdsong drifts down from high in the treetops and sounds more relaxed, less urgent than it did in springtime. The smell of pine and earth scent the air. Sunlight streams through small clearings in the trees, speckling the forest with patches of yellow sunlight. Broad flat rocks on river banks beckon, shining in the sun, places of quiet, solitude, and meditation.

At the beach and along the sea cliffs smiling families stroll, picnic, jump waves, and dig in the sand. Cool sea breezes brush hot, sunburned skin. Ice creams melt faster than children can eat them, running in vanilla and chocolate dribbles down sandy arms. Singles and lovers sunbathe, giggle, whisper secrets, and cavort in the sea. Others walk the shoreline lost in thought, or sit and look searchingly out to sea, as though looking for someone, or something, they've lost. Seashells and rocks are discovered, backs are warmed, and laughter mingles with the sound of the crashing waves and the cry of the sea birds.

It is summer.

By The Sea

Running, skipping, falling
Sand in your hair
Shouts and laughter ringing
Through the soft sea air
Breathing, feeling, *being*
No worries, just play
A break from the world
On a sunny salty day.

.

In Old Gougane

In old Gougane, that forest pristine,
Moss lays her carpet soft and green
Birdsong sweetly meets the ear
And the soft gurgling of water, running clear
Smooth stones revealed, colored, glistening
In old Gougane, the trees are listening.
Walking with footsteps easy and free
Along quiet ground there's only me
Breathing in the earthy fragrance sweet
The path forgiving beneath my feet
The hills caressed by the rising mist
The trees by the sun's golden light are kissed
And shadows play - or maybe faeries dancing?
Laughing, playing and romancing
I drink in the magic, the mystery, the peace
In old Gougane, one's soul does feast.

ENJOYING SUMMER: A beautiful blue-sky day, face painted in colorful designs and glitter, a shiny pink balloon which perfectly matches the favorite pink flowered skirt, and - just as soon as Mum finishes chatting - free ice cream moments away! What more could a girl want? [Kerry supermarket grand opening]

Recipes for Summer

Gougane Barra's Lemon Tart

Market Street Salmon

Thistlefield's Scones

Jameson Ginger & Lime

Happiness being a dessert so sweet
May life give you more than you can ever eat.
- Irish Blessing

GOUGANE BARRA LEMON TART *(P. 52)*

What says summer more perfectly than fresh lemons? There's nothing like enjoying a slice of Katy Lucey's Lemon Tart in the old-world elegance of the Gougane Barra Hotel, sitting in the elegant dining room overlooking Gougane Barra Lake. As I went on at some length about Gougane Barra in my last book, I'll curb myself here. Suffice it to say Katy and her husband Neil are superb hosts and two of my favorite people in Ireland. If you haven't been to the Gougane Barra Hotel, surely some day you will go. [Gouganebarrahotel.com] In the meantime, make this refreshing and tasty tart at home. Whether celebrating a special occasion - or just a lovely summer afternoon, why not serve it with a glass of sparkling wine? Or you could be truly Irish about it and give your guests both wine and tea. I enjoyed many a "tea in one hand and wine in the other" gathering in Ireland!

MARKET STREET SALMON *(P. 53)*

Ireland is known for its wonderful fresh seafood. If you don't happen to have an open air market up the street where a wellie boot and rubber glove wearing fishmonger holds court over a table gleaming with beautiful, just caught fish resting on mounds of ice, you can look elsewhere for your fresh salmon. This dish was often a part of the wonderful, bountiful more-dishes-than-you-can-count spreads Betty prepared for friends and family and it was always enjoyed by all.

THISTLEFIELD'S IRISH SCONES *(P. 55)*

Scones are something like biscuits, but if you call them that in Ireland they'll think you're talking about small cookies! This recipe is from a long-time American friend, Jan Tebbutt, a baker extraordinaire, and a frequent traveler to both England and Ireland, once the proprietress of a charming tea room, Thistlefields, in Gettysburg, Pennsylvania. She and her husband still carry on the tea tradition with a tea club and seasonal teas in the garden room of their home. While her husband is an Englishman, I've always thought of Jan as being far more Irish than English! Try her scone recipe and you will be, too!

JAMESON GINGER & LIME *(P. 57)*

A refreshing summer cocktail, and even if you aren't a whiskey drinker you'll likely enjoy it.

May the most you wish for be the least you get.
-Irish Toast

GOUGANE BARRA'S LEMON TART
Katy Lucy, Gougane Barra Hotel

If using pre-made cookie-crust or similar size pie shells, this will probably be enough to make two; otherwise should be more than enough for a deep dish crust or several individual tarts. Note different baking times depending on your tart size.

Ingredients:

7/8 C. superfine sugar
8 oz cream
4 eggs
juice of 2-3 lemons
zest of 1-2 lemons
sweet pastry case(s)

Directions:

1. Preheat oven to 325 deg. F.
2. Mix all ingredients together with hand whisk, but do not over-mix (i.e., not too many bubbles.)
3. Let rest, then fill pre-baked pastry case(s). Will be a very liquid mixture.
4. If making full-size tart, bake for 30 minutes, then decrease oven temp. to 300 deg. F. and bake another 10-15 min. For individual tarts, bake at 325 deg. F. for 10-15 minutes total.
5. Let cool before serving. Keep refrigerated.

Notes:

- This is very good - and easy - using a ready-made short-bread cookie crust. (Sh-h-h! Don't tell Katy!)

I closed my eyes and dreamed of summer and Gougane Barra...

MARKET STREET SALMON
Betty Jeffries

Easy to prepare, nutritious and delicious! You may use frozen salmon, but it's hard to beat fresh.

Ingredients:

salmon - preferably fresh - whole or side

6-8 heaping Tbspn butter

1/4-1/2 C white wine

a few sprigs of parsley

1-2 bay leaves

2-3 Tbspn lemon juice

salt and pepper

Directions:

1. Preheat oven to 325 deg. F.
2. Brush a large piece of foil with a little melted butter and place on a large baking sheet.
3. Place salmon in the center, sprinkle with salt and pepper to taste and splash a bit of white wine over the top.
4. Dot with several pats of butter, a few sprigs of parsley, a bay leaf or two, and a few squeezes of lemon juice.
5. Wrap the salmon loosely in the foil and seal well.
6. Place in preheated oven and cook about 10-15 min. per pound.
7. Serve garnished with sliced lemons and sprigs of fresh parsley.

Notes:

• When done, leave in foil to keep hot and moist before serving.

- Take care not to overcook or the fish will be dry. Cook only until it loses its translucent appearance.

According to Irish legend, the salmon is the fish of knowledge.

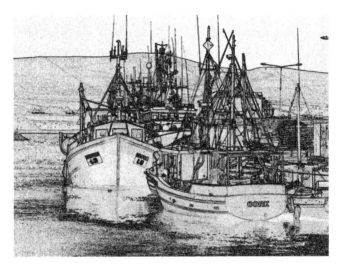

It's not a fish until it's on the bank.
- Irish Proverb

THISTLEFIELD'S IRISH SCONES
Jan Tebbutt

Jan is another weigher of dry ingredients and insists that's the only way to do it to insure consistency - and surely she knows better than I do! As with some of the other recipes, I've included both volume and weight measurements. Jan won't mind if you measure instead of weigh and, like my other contributors, if the recipe doesn't come out right she's far too kind to say, "I told you so!"

Ingredients:

16 oz [3.5 C + 2 Tbspn] all purpose flour

4 oz [1 stick or 1/2 C] butter, slightly soft (Kerrygold Irish butter recommended)

3 oz [1/3 C + 1 Tbspn, firmly packed] brown sugar

2 tspn baking powder

2 eggs beaten, room temperature

3 oz [just under 1/2 C] milk - when adding in, reserve a little.

Directions:

1. Preheat oven to 375 deg. F.
2. In a large bowl sift flour and rub in butter until it resembles bread crumbs.
3. Mix in brown sugar and baking powder. Use hands and/or wooden spoon to mix, and work quickly and lightly.
4. Mix in eggs and milk until dry ingredients form a soft dough. Add a little of the reserved milk if needed. Mix quickly and lightly; do not over mix.
5. Pat out on slightly floured surface to 1/2-3/4" thick and cut with floured scone cutter.

6. Place on baking sheet covered with parchment paper. Brush with a little milk and sprinkle with sugar (unless making savory option - see *Notes* below).
7. Bake for 8 minutes, then rotate baking sheet 180 deg. and continue baking another 4-7 minutes.
8. Best served warm with more of that good Irish butter - and a bit of jam would do no harm!

Notes:

- A food processor will quickly mix the flour and butter to breadcrumb consistency.
- Traditionally, Irish scones are more often cut into triangular pie-shaped pieces rather than rounds. Shape dough into a flattened circle and cut like you would a pie.
- These scones can be plain, sweet or savory. Try adding 1/2 C of raisins or other dried fruit, or chocolate bits/chips. For savory scones decrease the sugar to 1 Tbspn and add 1/2 tspn salt, then other ingredients such as 1/2 C grated cheddar or Parmesan cheese or a few tablespoons of dried herbs, or both.

What kind of scones did you bake today?

JAMESON GINGER & LIME

You may use any brand of whiskey you wish, but Jameson has my vote! Adjust measurements to your liking, using more or less ginger ale and lime.

Ingredients:

    ice
    Jameson or other good Irish whiskey
    ginger ale
    lime

Directions:

1. Fill a tall glass with ice.
2. Pour in 1 shot of whiskey and fill glass with ginger ale.
3. Squeeze a large wedge of lime into the glass, then drop it in. Stir. Feeling festive? Add a cherry!

Drink and enjoy!

*You never know the want of water
until the well has run dry - Irish Proverb*

AUTUMN

There is no fireside like your own fireside.

- Irish Proverb

When Irish stew is bubbling
And the soda bread is hot
and the Irish tea is steeping
In a little Irish pot,
When the room is warm with laughter
And the songs are bright and bold
And there's poetry and magic
In the stories that are told,
Isn't it a blessing, isn't it just grand
To know the heart and soul of you
Belongs to Ireland?

- Author Unknown

AUTUMN

*A*utumn: a last farewell to summer, a time of harvest, and preparation for winter. The sun's glow grows hazy, muted, its warmth beginning to wane.

In Ireland the term "fall" is not used at all, it is autumn, always autumn. But an Irish friend once mentioned to me how she found "fall" such a lovely Americanism.

The days begin to grow shorter and the evening air turns cooler, but many of summer's colors remain and warm temperatures some days can fool you into thinking it is still summer. The yellow gorse, bright reds and pinks of fuchsia, and patches of tall and graceful, orange montbretia still light up the green landscape, at least for a while. Autumn is a slow and gradual visitor.

One day a leaf drifts down from an overhead branch, lightly brushing your cheek, soft as a feather, landing at your feet. It is then you begin to notice autumn hues creeping in, gently covering those of summer.

Bright yellows become golden, from pale to deep, reds turn to darker, flaming russet, and splashes and streaks of orange and browns mix with the still mostly green fields. Hawthorns which bloomed so profusely in the May sunshine begin to show scarlet berries. The landscape is transformed from the wild, lush, brightness of summer to something more somber, but still beautiful.

Autumn leaves mixed with evergreens create a pretty canopy for a walk in the woods where the air smells clean and earthy. The deep, glossy green of holly seems more prominent. If you look closely, you might find brightly colored mushrooms growing in the darkest places, tucked in close to tree trunks and sheltered by curling ferns, making you wonder if you might soon come across Snow White and the Seven Dwarfs' cottage.

Even as we eat ice cream in the sunshine of an early autumn day, still tasting summer, old instincts seem to kick in, bringing the craving for hearty stews and other comfort foods, something signaling us from ancient times, telling us we must fatten up for the long cold winter ahead.

With luck the rains are soft and the winds are gentle, so the autumn leaves don't fall too soon. But eventually they do, as they must, drying and curling and gliding along the streets like little toy boats on a pond, skidding across the fields, and swirling around our ankles before the rains beat them into somber, sodden, forlorn little piles. Along with the now more visible branches on the trees, those small mounds of wet leaves become the signposts pointing toward winter.

The sheep are driven down from their summer mountain grazing grounds and thoughts and discussions turn to matters such as winter feed for livestock, weather predictions and warmer clothing.

Shop doors no longer stand open, closed against the cooler air, and merchandise is brought indoors. The sidewalk tables and chairs of pubs and cafes are stowed away and outdoor dining must wait until the first fine day of spring, one of those days when the air is still cool but filled with the playful teasing of summer.

Oil trucks cruise the streets, busy refilling home heating oil tanks. Gutters and downspouts are cleared, chimneys are cleaned, and bags of turf or bundles of turf briquettes are carted home. Woodpiles are assessed and truckloads of firewood delivered and stacked in out-buildings and back gardens.

Across the countryside the drone of chainsaws ripples the air as the last of the downed branches and trees, ignored since last winter's storms, are sawed and split into stove and fireplace-sized chunks, and woodpiles grow higher. If you are friends with the owner of one of those chainsaws, chances are you might find an empty feed sack filled with firewood (referred to as "timber") on your doorstep from time to time. It is very much the Irish way to share with friends and neighbors.

If the summer sun has been warm enough and frequent enough, wild blackberries have matured, ready to be plucked from their thorny vines for tarts and preserves, or simply eaten out of hand. The last of the potatoes are dug from the ground well before any chance of a freeze, and pumpkins and squash are harvested. Flowering bushes are pruned and flower bulbs planted, to hide in the earth through the cold of winter, to emerge in spring to delight not only the gardener but everyone who passes by.

Music in the pubs becomes less frequent but when it is heard, it is in some ways more enjoyable, a more intimate affair, as the main tourist crowds begin to thin and the locals once more become the majority.

Children and adults alike make Halloween plans. In town, shop windows are filled with ghosts and witches and hairy spiders sitting atop orange Jack-o-lanterns, creating a mix of eerie and whimsical displays illuminated with purple and orange lights. Posters advertise Halloween parades, bonfires, story telling, and haunted walks. Something for everyone, singles, couples, and families; the young, the older, the shy, the brave. Some jump right in and participate actively, others round up friends and family to enjoy an event, still others are solo, entertained by observing quietly from under the glow of a street lamp, or from the shelter and warmth of a pub doorway.

Home fires burn bright most evenings, giving warmth and cheer as the days grow ever shorter and the wind whispers, *winter is coming.* The kettle is always on for tea, cups more often filled, voices a little softer, and folks begin gathering nearer to the fire.

Autumn cradles and suspends us, a soft-spoken companion, gently easing us away from our midsummer night dreams and preparing us for winter.

Autumn

Gently, gently she comes
One of Mother Nature's children
Sent to help us
To ease us
To lightly touch our cheeks
And turn our faces
Away from summer
To distract us with her beautiful autumn colors
So that we might not miss summer
Quite so much.
So that we will remember, and sigh,
Then turn to the business at hand
And begin preparing
For winter.

You'll never plow a field
by turning it over in your mind.
-Irish Proverb

Recipes for Autumn

Dear Betty's Soda Bread

Irish Brown Bread

Bridget's Creamy Potato Soup

Bailey's Oatmeal

Derrynane Fresh Apple Cake

Half a loaf is better than no bread.
- Irish Proverb

DEAR BETTY'S SODA BREAD *(P. 70)*

Betty soon became known to me as "Dear Betty" whenever I thought of her, because she was (and is) just that: once a lovely neighbor and still a dear friend. She sometimes knocked on my back door, bringing me a smile and a loaf of her soda bread, still warm from the oven. She also served it at gatherings, sometimes held in the home where she grew up and learned how to bake from her mother in the old cooker, a large range with a door where wood is fed to the fire that heats cooking burners, oven, and indeed, sometimes the whole house. Now, you needn't have an old fashioned cooker to bake this bread, a modern oven will do quite nicely.

Betty would say of her own loaf, as she so often does about many of her dishes in her funny, self-deprecating way, "Oh, it's probably bloody awful!" It never is, of course - and if you follow her recipe, yours won't be, either!

IRISH BROWN BREAD *(P. 72)*

Philomena Kelly of Dublin, originally from Kenmare, kindly provided her family recipe for brown bread. I can neither make nor eat it without thinking of her smile, warmth, and entertaining quick wit. She and her partner Killian sometimes served this bread to those of us blessed to be invited to gatherings in their beautiful holiday home in Co. Kerry.

In fair weather we dined outdoors on the back deck overlooking the stretch of green lawn which slopes down to the river, the banks lined with tall trees. In spring, the hawthorns are heavy with white blossoms and lambs skip about in the adjoining field. In summer, bright flowers line the fence and dot the landscape, and the trees become a nearly solid wall of green.

When storms raged in winter, shaking the floor-to-ceiling windows and washing them with sheets of rain, we dined indoors by candlelight by a cheery fire, warm, cozy and safe.

BRIDGET'S CREAMY POTATO SOUP *(P. 73)*

This recipe comes from Bridget Haggerty, an Irish-American whose claim to fame is the wonderful Irish Culture & Customs website. I have long enjoyed the site, filled with a myriad of interesting and delightful things, among them this recipe for potato soup, sure to please on a crisp, cool autumn day.

BAILEY'S OATMEAL *(P. 75)*

I first enjoyed this dish at the Gougane Barra Hotel. It was served in a pretty china dish and accompanied by coffee in a silver pot, at a table draped in a white linen tablecloth with a tiny vase of fresh wildflowers in the center. The ambiance added to the experience, of course, but no matter where you are, if you want to eat or serve something decadently delicious to begin the day, I highly recommend this dish.

DERRYNANE FRESH APPLE CAKE *(P. 76)*

If you can't make it to Ireland to stay with Clare and Dezy at Thidwick, why not try Clare's apple cake recipe? While it's baking, pour yourself a cup of tea or coffee, sit back, relax and close your eyes...imagine you are sitting overlooking Derrynane Bay, the green hills behind you, the sun sparkling on the water... the sound of the waves crashing on the shore and the cries of soaring sea birds... the refreshing, clean scent of the coastal air... Wait! Don't let the apple cake burn!

The end of a feast is better than the beginning of a fight. - Irish Proverb

DEAR BETTY'S SODA BREAD
Betty Jeffries

Who doesn't like the smell of baking bread and what better time for it than autumn? Try Betty's bread with butter and jam, or cheese, or with any meal. Also delicious toasted! The below recipe is for brown (what Americans would call "wheat") soda bread. See Notes for white soda bread

Ingredients :

12 oz [about 2-1/2 C] whole wheat flour
4 oz [about 1 C] all-purpose flour
1 tspn superfine sugar
1 slightly rounded tspn baking soda
1 tspn salt
2-3 Tbspn melted butter
10-15 oz [1-1/4 to 1-7/8 C] buttermilk

Directions:

1. Preheat oven to 375 deg. F.
2. Mix all dry ingredients in a large bowl.
3. Make a well in the center, add butter, mix.
4. Add milk a little at a time, enough to make a soft dough but not too sticky. Mix lightly and quickly and do not over-mix.
5. Turn onto a floured work surface and bring together, kneading quickly a few times.
6. Pat the dough flat into a circle about 1.5" thick.
7. Make a fairly deep, large cross over the entire top of the bread with a floured knife and place on a floured or parchment-covered baking sheet.

8. Bake for 35-45 mins. When done, the loaf will sound slightly hollow when tapped on the base and a skewer or toothpick inserted in middle will come out clean. Cool on a wire rack.

Notes:

- For **white** soda bread: use all white flour (16 oz, or 3-1/2 C) and delete butter. All other ingredients are the same.

- Betty says her mother sometimes added sultanas (similar to raisins) as a treat to the white bread ingredients before adding the milk.

It's easy to imagine the six little O'Sullivan children gathered around the table by the old cooker that still dominates the space today, the room filled with the aroma of freshly baked soda bread. Smiling and giggling, their eyes dance with pleasure and mischief and their feet with the desire to go back outdoors to play, the only thing holding them the knowledge that in moments they'll be eating a warm slice of soda bread slathered in butter.

*Every mother thinks
it is for her own child the sun rises.*
- Irish Proverb

IRISH BROWN BREAD
Philomena Kelly

This bread is delicious and remarkably easy to make. As with Dear Betty's Soda Bread, this bread pairs well with just about anything and is also excellent on its own.

Ingredients:

16 oz [3-1/2 C] wholewheat flour
1-3/8 C. pinhead oatmeal (may use regular oatmeal)
2 large "fists" (about 1/2 C total) of bran
2 level Tbspn, packed, dark brown sugar
2 tspn salt
2 tspn baking soda
3 C buttermilk

Directions:

1. Preheat oven to 400°F and grease two 1-lb loaf tins.
2. Mix all dry ingredients.
3. Make well in center and add buttermilk. Hand mix. (Will be a fairly liquid mixture, something like cake batter, not like bread dough.)
4. Pour into loaf tins and bake for approx. 1 hour.
5. Bread is done when toothpick inserted near center comes out clean. Cool on wire rack before slicing.

There is something both comforting and satisfying about the making and eating of good bread.

BRIDGET'S CREAMY POTATO SOUP

Bridget Haggarty, IrishCultureandCustoms.com

Bridget makes her own chicken stock but if you're lazy like me or simply out of time, canned will do in a pinch!

Ingredients:

1/2 C (1 stick) unsalted butter
1 C onions, thinly sliced
1 C leeks, thinly sliced
4 C potatoes, peeled and sliced
6 C chicken stock
1 tspn salt
20 turns freshly ground black pepper
1/2 C grated cheddar cheese
4 slices crisp-cooked bacon, drained and crumbled
1/2 C fresh chives, chopped

Directions:

1. Melt the butter in a large heavy pot over low heat.
2. Add the onions and leeks and stir to cover them with butter.
3. Cover the pot and cook slowly to allow the vegetables to sweat - about 20 minutes.
4. Add the potatoes, stir into the butter, cover the pot, and cook over low heat another 15 minutes.
5. Stir in the stock, salt, and pepper.
6. Increase the heat to medium-high until soup begins to bubble, then reduce heat and simmer until the potatoes are tender, 20 to 30 minutes.
7. In a food processor or blender, puree the soup in batches and return it to the pot. Heat thoroughly.
8. Serve garnished with cheddar cheese, bacon and chives.

Notes:

- If you want a chunkier, heartier main dish soup, skip the blender and mash and stir well by hand, then add 2 cups cooked potatoes cut into small chunks and/or diced cooked ham.

A delicious soup for a brisk autumn day!

*Here's to eyes in your head
and none in your spuds!*
- Irish Toast

BAILEY'S OATMEAL

In Ireland, oatmeal is known as porridge, or porridge oats. Surprise a loved one with this treat for a special occasion, or enjoy it yourself. No one can argue it wouldn't be a unique and tasty "top o' the mornin'" way to start the day, no matter what you call it! The recipe is for one serving.

Ingredients:

Oatmeal of your choice, cooked to your liking
1/8-1/4 C chocolate chips
1-2 oz Bailey's Irish Cream

Directions:

Pour cooked oatmeal into a bowl. Pour a jigger or two of Bailey's Irish Cream over the top and sprinkle with chocolate chips.

After eating a bowl of this, don't be surprised if you hear a wee Irish lilt in your voice!

*Let broth boil slowly,
but let porridge make a noise.*
- Irish Saying

♣

DERRYNANE FRESH APPLE CAKE
Clare Smith

Autumn is apple season. This cake is a delicious way to use them!

Ingredients:

1 C vegetable oil

2 C granulated white sugar

3 eggs

2 tspn vanilla

1/2 tspn salt

3 C flour

1 tspn baking soda

1 C chopped nuts (walnuts and/or pecans)

3 C chopped apples (preferably Bramley or Granny Smith)

For Glaze: 1 C light brown sugar
1/2 C [1 stick] butter
1/4 C cream
1 tspn vanilla

Directions:

1. Preheat oven to 350°F. (or 325°F - see step 7.)
2. Grease 9 x 13 baking pan or grease and flour 10" tube pan
3. Combine oil and white sugar, beat well.
4. Add eggs and vanilla. Set aside.
5. In a separate bowl, sift together flour, salt and baking soda, then add to oil mixture.
6. Stir in nuts and apples.

7. Bake in 9x13 pan for 40-45 mins. at 350°F, or in 10" tube pan at 325°F for about 1 hour.

<u>Glaze</u>: (make while cake is baking so ready when cake is done)
  1. Heat brown sugar & butter, stirring until melted.
  2. Add cream, continue stirring, and bring to full boil (the sugar will dissolve at this stage), then remove from heat.
  3. Cool and stir in vanilla.
  4. As soon as cake is out of the oven, pierce with fork in several places and pour glaze evenly over warm cake.

You know what they say about an apple a day? Well, no one said it couldn't be in a cake!

If you do not sow in the spring,
you will not reap in the autumn.
- Irish Proverb

Your feet will bring you to where your heart is.
- Irish Proverb

DID YOU KNOW?

WHERE YA' FROM? In 2013, 33.3 million Americans claimed to have Irish ancestry (census.gov), more than six times the population of Ireland. In Ireland, most of the 4.76 million people are Irish-born. Only about 5,000 of the 79,000 non-Irish are Americans. (cso.ie).

FANCY SOME CORNED BEEF & CABBAGE? Contrary to popular American belief, you'd be hard-pressed to find corned beef & cabbage on a restaurant menu in Ireland. This is not a traditional Irish dish, but it is most definitely an Irish-American dish.

Millions of Irish immigrated to the United States starting in the late 1700's and brought with them their own food traditions. Except during the famine, pork and potatoes were often a standard part of meals in Ireland, but immigrants found pork was too expensive in America.

Living among other ethnic groups, the Irish discovered corned beef found in Jewish delis. Cured and cooked something like Irish bacon, corned beef became the replacement for the pork they could no longer afford. Cooked with cabbage, readily available and cheaper than potatoes, it became an inexpensive and tasty dish. While many no doubt longed for the green fields, pork and potatoes, and Irish stew of their homeland, corned beef and cabbage eventually became a popular and common meal in Irish American homes.

CHEERS! Uisce beatha, the Irish word for whiskey, means "water of life."

CHIPS OR CRISPS? In Ireland, if you want potato chips, ask for crisps. If you want french fries, it's chips you're after.

AH, THE PUB'S CLOSED! There are only two days in Ireland when law requires pubs to be closed and alcohol is not sold anywhere: Good Friday and Christmas Day. St. Patrick's Day, also a religious holiday, was the third day on this list for several decades. That law was repealed across Ireland in the 1970's. On Good Friday, pubs serving food can remain open and serve alcohol if the customer is also ordering food.

WILL YOU HAVE A CUPPA? Think the English are the biggest tea drinkers? Ireland ranks ahead of England and is one of the biggest per capita tea drinking nations in the world. Tea is an important part of the culture. When you are a guest in someone's home, a cup of tea is always offered. It is as much a part of the greeting ritual as saying "Hello, how're ya' keepin'?"

THE PERFECT PINT. According to Guinness, it takes 119.5 seconds to pour a proper pint of Guinness: tilt the glass at a 45 deg. angle, fill to 3/4 full, then let sit until the bubbles have risen to the top and formed a head, then fill the rest of the way. Sadly, many American bartenders seem quite unfamiliar with this technique!

'TIS RAININ'! Sure everyone knows it rains in Ireland. But according to Met Eireann, the highest recorded rainfall for one day occurred on September 18, 1993, at Cloonee Lake in County Kerry. A whopping 243.5 mm - more than *9.5 inches* - fell on that day! (met.ie)

May the rocks in your fields turn to gold.
- Irish Blessing

Chroí agus Anam

Some day I'll go back again
To see what the eye can see
Back again to Ireland,
My heart, my soul, and me.
Back again to see the sun,
The sun that shines so bright
And watch the sky change colors
As day slips into night.
Back again to see the stars
That stud the velvet sky
Back again to feel the wind
Wrap me in a comforting sigh.
Back again to walk along
The damp and quiet streets
Splashing through rain puddles
Wellie boots upon my feet.
Back again to wave hello
To familiar faces now so dear
To gaze upon a rainbow
Through a sky washed crystal clear.
Yes, some day we'll go back again
My heart, my soul and me
Back to dear old Ireland
Where we've so longed to be.

Chroí agus Anam: Heart and Soul

May you never forget what is worth remembering,
or remember what is best forgotten. - *Irish Blessing*

RECIPE NOTES

I confess I haven't tried making all of these recipes, but I have sampled most of the them and they were excellent. Like many good cooks and bakers everywhere, some of my contributors are accustomed to a "pinch" of this and a "handful" of that when cooking, rather than specific measurements. Others weigh their ingredients. To further complicate matters, some measurements are different than those used in the USA (e.g., liters versus quarts, 20 oz versus 16 oz pint), baking temperatures were in Celsius, and ingredients were named differently (e.g., bread soda versus baking soda). "Superfine" sugar is called for in some recipes. Regular granulated sugar will work, but superfine is what the recipe specifies. All in all, translating the recipes into "American" was more complicated than I anticipated. Ah, well, at least they weren't in the Irish language! If something doesn't come out quite as you'd hoped the first time, try it again, adjusting time, temperature, and perhaps some of the ingredients to your taste. And while you're at it, have fun, won't you?

Jane and Betty at Mick & Jimmy's, Kenmare, Ireland (2016)

*What is more pleasant than gathering together
to drink, dine and laugh with friends?*

To all the days here and after
May they be filled with fond memories,
Happiness, and laughter.
-Irish Blessing

RECIPE INDEX

Breads
Dear Betty's Soda Bread - 70
Irish Brown Bread - 72

Cakes
Chocolate Guinness Cake - 36
Derrynane Fresh Apple Cake - 76
O'Sullivan's Christmas Pudding - 16
Liz's Porter Cake - 12

Drinks
Hot Whiskey - 19
Irish Coffee - 18
Jameson Ginger & Lime 57

Soups & Stews
Beef & Guinness Stew - 14
Bridget's Creamy Potato Soup - 73
Clare's Irish Stew - 33

Other
Bailey's Oatmeal - 75
Colcannon - 35
Gougane Barra's Lemon Tart - 52
Market Street Salmon - 53
Pendy's Potato Cakes - 32
Thistlefield's Irish Scones - 55

If at first you don't succeed, try, try again.
- Thomas H. Palmer, The Teacher's Manual (1840)

PHOTOS

Except where noted, all photos taken in and around Kenmare, Co. Kerry, Ireland.

Cover: Tree-lined wall near Tralee Town Park and Rose Garden, Tralee, Co. Kerry.

Intro Pages: Sheep farmers in The Square; Henry Street and Holy Cross steeple; Dingle Peninsula fields, Co. Kerry; Ring of Kerry road signs, Iveragh Peninsula.

Winter: Home fire on Market Street; winter tree on Cromwell Court; bird and celtic cross, Clonmacnoise, Co. Offaly; winter trees in back garden; Cafe Mocha sidewalk sign; young boy joins music session at Coachman's pub; Guinness sign, Blind Piper Pub, Caherdaniel, Co. Kerry; candles against the gloom; Irish coffee; cottage ruin on Beara Peninsula; new wood stove and old horseshoe.

Spring: Sheep and lamb near Finnihy River; mare and colt near Derrynane, Co. Kerry; cow and calf on Kilgarvan road; wild daisies, Brú na Bóinne, Co. Meath; musicians at McCarthy's Pub; Kenmare market baked goods; Carriganass Castle, West Cork; shamrocks; O'Connor's Guinness keg table; Kenmare Bay from Reenagross Park.

Summer: Hydrangeas in bloom; Henry Street; Betty by the sea, Beara Peninsula; Gougane Barra Forest.; little girl enjoying summer; lake view from Gougane Barra Hotel dining room; Tom Crean's Restaurant; fishing boats, Dingle Bay; rose in Tralee Rose Garden, Co. Kerry; Jameson barrel at Jameson Distillery, Dublin; farmers and cows, Kenmare Fair Day; musicians at O'Murchu's.

Autumn: Fuchsia bushes and hills in Glenbeigh, Co. Kerry; my tea pot; autumn leaves; musicians at Crowley's Pub; sheep on Healy Pass, Beara Peninsula; coffee at Mick & Jimmy's; ready for dinner guests; tea and biscuits; Ha'Penny Bridge and building reflections in River Liffey, Dublin; St. Finbarr's Church and Gougane Barra Lake.

Closing Pages: 81- Heart ornament from The White Room.
82- Glendalough, Co. Wicklow and MacCarthy's Bar, Castletownberehaven, Beara Peninsula.
84- Molly Gallivan's cottage, Sheen Valley, Co. Kerry.

ABOUT THE AUTHOR

Forced to return to the USA after almost three years in Ireland because of a change in Ireland's immigration policy, Jane Fadely counts those days in County Kerry among some of the very best of her life.

Frequently moved to write about her experiences and observations while in Ireland, she continues to be inspired by her memories of the place she once called home.

Jane plans to settle in western North Carolina soon and hopes she might find some similarities between the mountain culture there and the life she enjoyed in Ireland.

A sequel to her book, *Chickens in the Garden, Wellies by the Door: An American in Rural Ireland,* is in progress with an anticipated release date in late 2017.

Personalized/signed copies of *Seasons of Ireland* and *Chickens in the Garden* may be purchased through IREUSA Press (ireusapress@gmail.com).

Please visit::
- FACEBOOK.COM/VJFADELY
- GOUGANEBARRAHOTEL.COM
- IRELANDUNPLUGGEDTOURS.COM
- IRISHCULTUREANDCUSTOMS.COM

Like the gold of the sun,
Like the light of the day,
May the luck of the Irish
Shine bright on your way.
Like the glow of a star,
And the lift of a song
May these be your joys
All your life long.

- *Irish Blessing*

46715004R00056

Made in the USA
Middletown, DE
08 August 2017